VOLLEYBALL
ADVANCED SKILLS AND STRATEGIES

ZACHARY A. KELLY

The Rourke Corporation, Inc.
Vero Beach, Florida 32964

PHOTO CREDITS:
All photos © Tony Gray

Illustration page 24 © East Coast Studios

PROJECT EDITORIAL SERVICES:
David Jones, Connie Deninberg

EDITORIAL SERVICES:
Penworthy Learning Systems

Library of Congress Cataloging-in-Publication Data

Kelly, Zachary A., 1970-
    Volleyball—advanced skills and strategies / Zachary A. Kelly.
        p. cm. — (Volleyball)
    Includes index.
    Summary: Presents skills and strategies for more advanced volleyball players, including such topics as specialization, simple and multiple offense, advanced spiking, defense, and blocking techniques.
    ISBN 0-86593-502-5
    1. Volleyball—Juvenile literature. [1. Volleyball.] I. Series: Kelly, Zachary A., 1970-   Volleyball.
QV1015.3.K436 1998
796.325—dc21   98–8565
                                                                                     CIP
                                                                                     AC

Printed in the USA

TABLE OF CONTENTS

Good form will help you perform a perfect overhead serve.

TEAMWORK

Before you can play well as a team member, you have to be consistent in your basic skills. Basic volleyball skills include serving and performing **forearm** and **overhead passes**, **attacks**, **digs**, and **emergency techniques**.

Every player serves the ball in volleyball. A good serve can give your team an offensive advantage or earn your team quick points. A poor serve keeps your team on the defense. The forearm and overhead pass are also important offensive moves to learn.

If a player passes well, teammates can depend on him or her during a play. Attacking, too, is an offensive technique of good team players. A good **attacker** can disarm an opposing team or earn the winning point.

For defense, each player must perform the dig consistently. This motion is crucial anywhere on the court, but especially on the back line. One good dig can turn the play from defense to offense for a team. Players also must perform emergency techniques well to save the ball for their team. Team players are well-rounded; they have all these skills—and more.

Playing Your Position

Once you can perform the basics consistently, you are ready to use them in a game. In a volleyball game, you will not only perform the actions but also work for your team in your assigned position.

Each play begins with the teammates on both sides in rotational order. As soon as the server contacts the ball, players move to their playing positions. If your team has not specialized, you play whatever position you are currently at in the rotation. If your team is specialized, you will move to your position on the court at the moment the server contacts the ball.

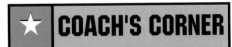

★ COACH'S CORNER

A fast way to improve your skills is to listen to your coach or a player who is more advanced than you—and follow his or her advice.

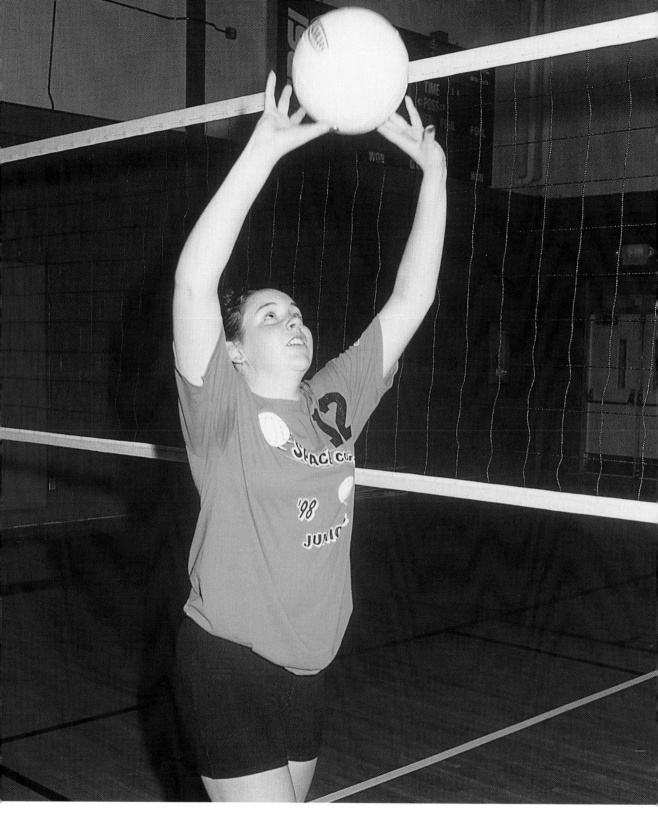

A front court player sets the ball.

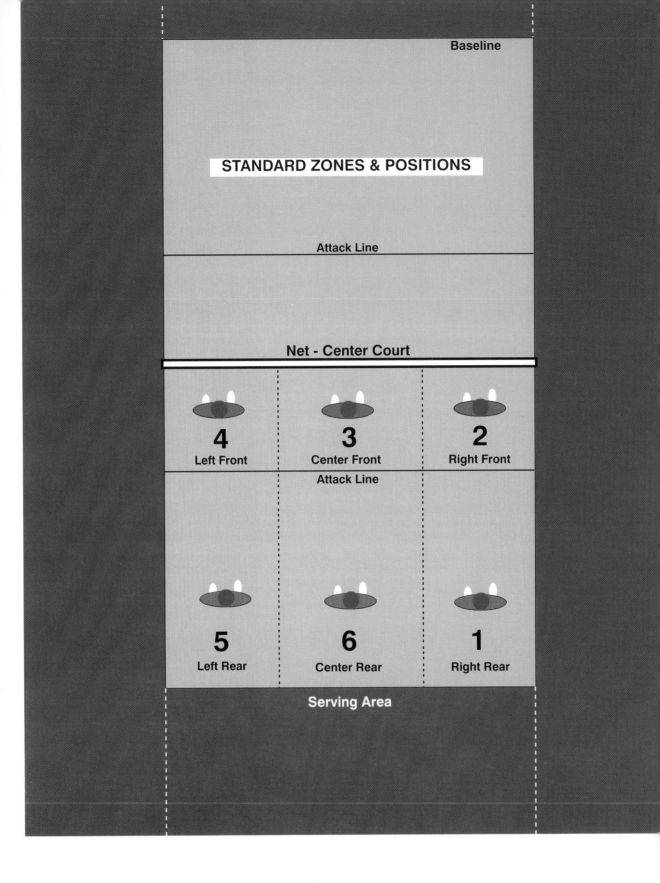

Baseline

STANDARD ZONES & POSITIONS

Attack Line

Net - Center Court

4	3	2
Left Front	Center Front	Right Front

Attack Line

5	6	1
Left Rear	Center Rear	Right Rear

Serving Area

8

However your coach organizes your team, playing your position is important.

Front court players mostly block, **set**, and attack the ball. **Back court** players usually dig, pass, and receive it. At times a back court player will reach into the front court to support a play or to keep the ball off the floor.

Working Together

Once team members play their positions well, they can take advantage of each player's position to make good plays. If the ball is coming into your range of effectiveness, call for it. If the ball is in the other team's court and it looks like it will be a free ball, call it. These calls help other players prepare their actions and support yours. When you're involved in a play, stay in your position so teammates will know where you are. Any time you're playing the ball, be aware of the **setter**. The setter is the key person for a player receiving the ball and for the attacker. When you are not involved in a play, your job is to support your teammates who are. When a teammate receives the ball, open yourself to it. Face that teammate with your shoulder and hips toward the ball. Be in ready position, prepared to join the play if needed.

COACH'S CORNER

Use your voice often. Communicating with your teammates may be the edge you'll need to win.

Team Strategies

Beginning teams use different strategies than intermediate and advanced teams. They organize their play differently. Players just learning the game of volleyball need practice in basic skills. They are also learning to play their positions. Coaches usually stress these basics, and do not specialize or develop advanced strategies. Instead, they work on simple strategies and train the team to work together.

This team starts each practice using basic skills as a warmup.

A coach slams the ball to help these players perfect a double block.

As you can guess, an intermediate or advanced team uses more complex plans than beginners. Most intermediate teams specialize by assigning an offensive role to each player. Every player is either an attacker or a setter. Specialization narrows a player's role. With fewer decisions to make during play, most players will play better.

Advanced teams plan detailed strategies for defense and offense. They consider the strengths and weaknesses of each player and give every teammate a position and a role for each play. On advanced teams, players and their coach often analyze plans before a game and mistakes afterwards. They're always looking for ways to improve their teamwork. If you get an opportunity, ask someone to videotape a practice or game. Study the way you play and your team plays. See if you can find mistakes and correct them before the next game.

SPECIALIZATION

Most sports separate offense and defense. Some sports change players when they move from offense to defense. Some sports even change equipment. In other sports, though, the distinction between offense and defense is much smaller. Volleyball has offensive and defensive plays. But, a player often uses both in one play. He or she might **block** (defense) an attack and **tip** (offense) the ball back over in one play.

To solve the problem of learning offensive and defensive moves for all six positions, many teams specialize. A player is assigned one back court and one front court position. For example, when the rotation puts you in the back court, you might always play the center back position. Advanced teams also assign the role of setter or attacker to each player. Specializing allows players to master two positions, rather than learning a little about six positions.

Front Court

Front court players run a team's offense. They also carry some key defensive duties. These players attack, block, and dink (tip), handling any ball that is playable within their range of effectiveness. To be good in the front court, players follow these guidelines.

Front court players usually do not hit a ball coming at them at chest height or higher. (As it travels to the back court, the ball will drop. Ball control will be easier for a back court player.) If a front court player can receive the ball with an overhead pass, however, he or she might take it. Front court players are always ready to set, attack, or block.

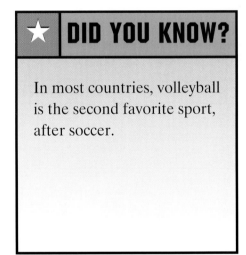

★ **DID YOU KNOW?**

In most countries, volleyball is the second favorite sport, after soccer.

These front court players jump to block the ball.

A middle court player digs to set up an attack.

Defensively, front court players keep their hands at or above shoulder height and they stay close to the net. On a block, they reach far across the net, avoiding contact with it.

Back Court

Back court players support the front. They cover any ball past the front court and often play defense. Back court players frequently use forearm passes, digs, and emergency techniques. To move quickly from defense to offense, back court players follow a few important guidelines.

Back court players allow any ball coming to them at or above chest height or higher to pass. Balls that high in the back court will almost always go out. The middle back player often covers the middle of the court, leaving the deepest area to the right and left players. The left court position is the more aggressive position if the ball comes between the two outside back court players.

Defensively, back court players stay in a low body position with their weight forward. They also watch closely in case they need to make an emergency move. Back court players on the sideline also call the ball for players in front of them if it is going out of bounds.

17

Setters and Attackers

Most advanced teams assign the role of setter or attacker to each teammate. This offensive role allows the players to specialize in one part of the attack so that they can perform it very well in front or back court. The better the individuals perform their responsibilities, the better the offense of the entire team. The best spiker on a team is useless if he or she does not get a good set.

This back court player uses a forearm pass to receive the ball.

This player begins a back-set with her back arched and her arms
in the air.

Setters follow these unwritten "rules" to help them set an effective attack. A setter should never receive a serve, since he or she cannot hit the ball two times in a row. Instead, setters often "hide" at the net or behind another player so that they will be open to set the attack. A setter also calls short serves that will not make it over the net, and the setter calls free balls. Finally, the setter decides who will attack by setting to that player. A second ball played on a side is always played by the setter.

Attackers also have unwritten "rules." An attacker can serve, receive, or dig the ball to the setter. The attacker watches the play and works with the setter to prepare an attack. The attacker will "read" the blockers and decide the most effective form of attack—spike, half spike, or tip.

SIMPLE OFFENSE AND SERVE RECEPTION

When players have mastered basic skills, it is time to organize their moves on the court. It is also time to assign positions. A plan for assigning a certain place and role to each player is called a "formation."

Players work together in formation to send the ball over. In volleyball, there are offensive and **defensive formations**.

Offensive formations may be simple or multiple. The difference between them is the position of the setter and the number of setters on the court.

When the setter is in the front court, the formation is a **simple offensive** formation. A simple offense has two attackers and a setter at the net. The setter often plays front right and can set to either the attacker on the left or in the middle. In a **multiple offensive** formation, the setter plays offense (sets) out of the front row, but goes to the back row to play defense. Most teams begin with the simple offense.

4-2 Offense and 4-2 International Offense

Offensive formations usually have numbers such as 4-2 for names. The first number indicates how many attackers are in the formation; the second number, how many setters. A 4-2 formation has four attackers and two setters. The setters are opposite each other in rotation so that one of them is always in the front row at the net. The front court setter is the primary setter in this formation.

The 4-2 formation is the most common system for beginning teams. In a 4-2, the setter plays the center right front position. Attackers play the left and right front positions. This formation is easier for the setter since he or she can pass to either side.

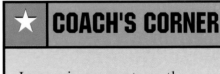

★ **COACH'S CORNER**

Improving your strength helps prevent injury. Exercise, lift weights, and play to help improve your body's strength.

A player spikes a ball from this simple offense.

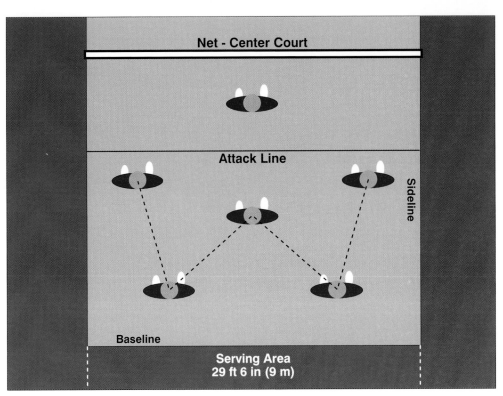

"W" Formation

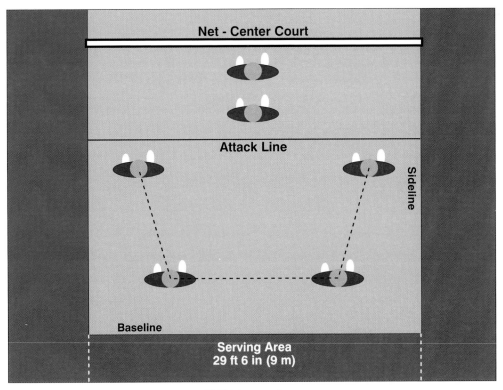

"U" Formation

24

The other type of simple offense is also a 4-2 offense. It is the International 4-2. In this system, the setter plays the right front position. If the setter is right handed, this means he or she is passing to his or her strong side. This gives the setter more power and control. The International 4-2 is slightly more difficult to learn, but offers an advantage to the setter.

The Serve Receive

There are several common patterns teams use to receive a serve. These patterns work for simple and for multiple offensive formations. Two serve reception patterns are named after the letters of the alphabet they resemble. They are the five-person **"W" pattern** and the four-person **"U" pattern**.

In the "W" pattern, five players receive the serve. The front court setter "hides" at the net until the serve. At contact, the setter moves away from the net and into playing position. The left and right back court players cover the two deep points of the "W." The front court attackers cover the outer front court points, and the center back player covers the middle front point. This pattern keeps the setter from receiving the serve and leaves him or her open to set the attack.

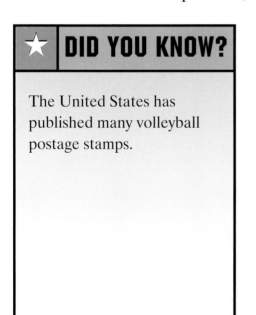

★ DID YOU KNOW?

The United States has published many volleyball postage stamps.

In the "U" pattern, the server and one other player are hidden from the serve-receive, and the remaining four players form a "U-shaped" pattern to receive the serve. In two-person and three-person patterns, two or three players line up in the back court to receive the serve. By choosing different serve-receive formations, you allow your best passers to receive the serve.

A good offensive formation helps a team cover the attacker and receive a free ball. Changing the simple offensive formation can turn the play into a great attack for your team.

Players shift positions to cover an attack.

Protected by her pads, this player goes for an emergency save.

When an attacker attacks, the ball may hit the opponent's floor; the other team may make a dig; or they may block the ball. If the opponent blocks and the ball comes back over the net, it may hit the floor. To prevent this, a team "covers" the attacker. The setter and the other front court attacker move to the right and left of the attacker. The center back player moves between them. In a low-body position, the three cover the attacker in a semi-circle during the attack.

If the other team does not have enough control of the ball to complete their attack, they may send an easy ball over. This is a free ball. When an incomplete attack comes in the form of a free (easy) ball, the receiving team should go into the "W" formation with the setter already in place. The attackers or back row players receive; the setter makes the set; and the attacker sends it over.

MULTIPLE OFFENSE AND SERVE RECEPTION

Multiple Offense

After a team perfects its simple offense, it can begin learning multiple offenses. Multiple offenses are much stronger than simple ones, but they are more difficult to do. For a team to learn multiple offenses all six players must be able to attack and at least four players must be able to spike strongly and consistently. Teams without this level of skill should stay with simple offenses, like the 4-2.

The two main multiple offenses are the 6-2 and the 5-1. In a 6-2 formation, all six players are attackers; but two of the six players are also setters. Two setters make it possible to place a setter in the backcourt for all six rotations. In a 5-1 formation, all players are attackers; but only one player is a setter. The 5-1 has its setter in the back court for three rotations and in the front court for three rotations. The big advantage of multiple offense is the powerful front court and the ability to run different types of sets. When the setter is in the back row, all three front court players can attack. When the setter is in the front row, the other two players can attack and so can the setter if necessary.

The 6-2 and 5-1 in Detail

Again, all players in the 6-2 are attackers and two are setters. The setters are opposite each other in rotation. Thus, the active setter will always be in the back court and come to the net to set. The front court setter works mostly as an attacker instead of a setter. Since the server almost always comes from the back court, the front three players are free to attack in many ways. This flexibility of attack is the 6-2 formation's greatest strength. Another strength is the front court setter. He or she usually attacks but can also set. The 6-2 offense, then, gives the team many attack options.

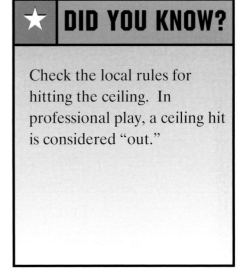

★ **DID YOU KNOW?**

Check the local rules for hitting the ceiling. In professional play, a ceiling hit is considered "out."

This play shows a quick set and attack from a 6-2 offense.

This back court player prepares for a dig.

The 5-1 formation is the most common international offense. The 5-1 has only one setter, but it remains nearly as flexible as the 6-2. For the rotations when the setter is in the back court, all three front court players can attack. When the setter moves to the front court, he or she can use the position strategically. Instead of setting every time, the setter can occasionally attack on the second ball contact. This move puts the other team off their guard. A big advantage of the 5-1 is its single setter. With only one setter, the team can count on consistency in timing and placement of the set.

Receiving a Serve

Multiple offense uses the three-person, two-person, "W," and "U" patterns with a few changes. The changes are designed to keep the setter from accidentally receiving the serve. Since the setter is in the back row instead of the front, the setter hides behind another player to avoid receiving. The center back player usually moves to the right to cover the setter's area. Any of the front row players may receive the serve in multiple patterns.

In the "W" formation, the setter hides behind a front court player during the serve. The moment the server contacts the ball, the setter moves quickly into position between the center and right front players.

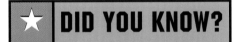

DID YOU KNOW?

If a ball lands on a line, the ball is considered "in." The sidelines and end lines are part of the court.

The setter hides in the "U" formation as well. If the setter is in the front row in the 5-1 formation, he or she may act as an attacker with the real attacker hiding behind the setter. When the serve begins, the real attacker receives the ball.

Covering the Attacker and Free Ball Formation

The formations for covering the attacker look the same in multiple and simple offense formations. The difference is the position each player covers in the pattern. In multiple offense, the setter takes the middle place in the semicircle around the attacker, while the center forward takes the position closest to the net.

This team is prepared to receive the ball from a two-person pattern.

A well-executed forearm pass.

In the simple offense formations, the center back takes the middle position and the two front court players take the right and left sides. If the setter is in the front row of a 5-1 formation, however, the team usually follows the 4-2 offensive pattern.

The free ball formation in multiple offense is quite different from simple offense formations. First, the setter must move from the back court to the net. In simple formations, the setter is already there. Secondly, all three front court players move off the net to the attack line. Finally, the center back player moves to the right in this formation to cover the setter's area. If the setter is in the front court in the 5-1 formation, the team uses the simple offensive pattern.

DEFENSIVE FORMATIONS

Defensive Strategy

Volleyball uses several defense formations : 2-1-3, 2-4, perimeter, and rotation. The 2-1-3 is flexible and simple to perform but is not very effective against hard-driven spikes. Its strength is its effectiveness against off-speed attacks and tips. The 2-4 defense is more complicated but coverage in the deep backcourt—where hard spikes usually land—make it strong against hard-driven spikes.

Perimeter and rotation defenses also have strengths and weaknesses. It is your coach's responsibility to choose a defense that is effective against your opponent. Most teams learn 2-1-3 defenses first because it's simple and strong against beginning and intermediate teams. A good strategy is to learn both formations, then use the one that works best against a given opponent.

Whichever formation a team uses, three skills are always important. First, all team members must be able to read what the opponent is about to do. Second, all team members must be able to use the information to position themselves defensively. Third, team members must receive the attack and move immediately to an offensive position. The best way to learn these skills is through coaching, practice, and experience.

The 2-1-3 Formation

Carrying out 2-1-3 defenses requires learning three positions: the base, the free-ball, and the block. The base position is the starting point of the 2-1-3. In base position, the two attackers and the setter remain at the net. The center back player stays in the center midcourt, and the remaining two players stay in just behind the 10 foot line and near the sidelines.

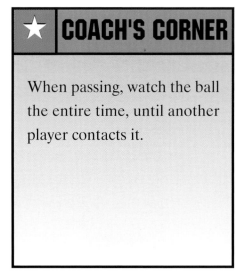

★ COACH'S CORNER

When passing, watch the ball the entire time, until another player contacts it.

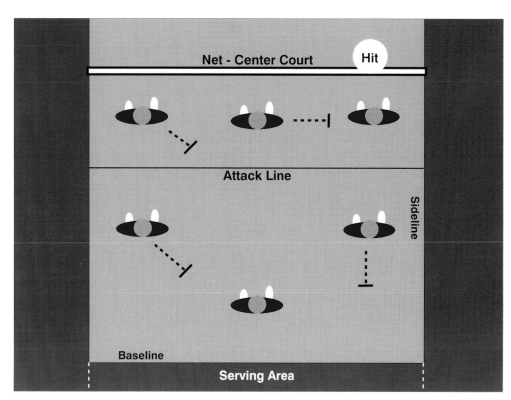

Perimeter Defence

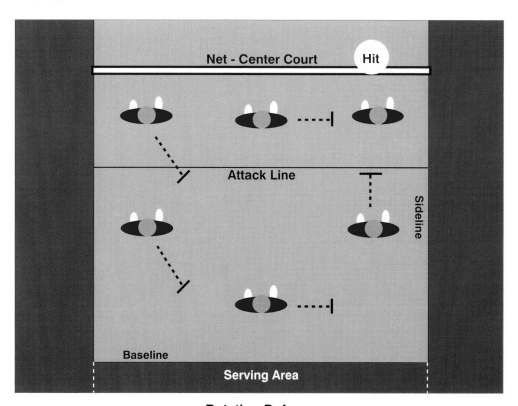

Rotation Defense

39

After this spike, the team will immediately take their defensive positions.

Players hold this position until the team leader calls "free ball" or "block," signaling the team to move to one of the other 2-1-3 positions.

Movement to free-ball position is simple. The right and left forward players move back just behind the attack line, and the center forward stays at the net. The center back player moves forward to the attack line, and the right and left backcourt players move back and in a few feet. This change of position gives the team better coverage for receiving a free ball. The team is also ready to shift into strong offense. This positioning will depend on whether the setter is on the back or front row.

Block positions are harder. Three positions are possible, depending on which opposing team member is spiking. The key is to double block, or position two blockers in the area where the ball is expected to land. If the opposing right forward spikes, the center front court player should move to block with the left front player. At the same time, the setter should move back to the 10 foot line ready to dig. If the opposing left forward spikes, the middle front joins the right front player to block. An attack from the opposing center forward requires the center front court player to move to block.

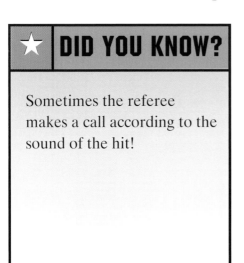

★ DID YOU KNOW?

Sometimes the referee makes a call according to the sound of the hit!

The 2-4 Formation

The 2-4 defense also uses base, free-ball, and block positions. In base position, the three forward players stay close to the net. The center backcourt player moves all the way to the endline. The right and left backcourt players remain midway between the attack line and the endline, but they move a few feet in toward the center of the court. This move helps protect the center midcourt. Players hold this formation until a team leader calls "free ball" or "block."

This spike attempt ended up as a free ball for the other team.

Missing a block can cost your team a point.

The 2-4 free-ball formation is much like 2-1-3 free-ball formation. The centerback moves forward to the attack line, and the right and left back court players move back and in a few more feet. The right and left forwards move to the attack line, and the center forward stays at the net. Players can then receive the ball and move quickly into an offense formation.

Block positions for the 2-4 defense are also similar to those in the 2-1-3 defense. Double blocking is again the key.

The Perimeter Defense

This defense shifts players to cover the more common left side hits. The goal is to cover the perimeter of the court.

The middle front player shifts to help cover the right front position and a possible block. Other players will also shift to this side of the court. This adds four diggers to cover the serve and greater flexibility. The main weakness of this defense is that it does not cover tips well and leaves holes in the center and back left corner of the court.

The Rotation Defense

The rotation defense is a great defense against tips. Its purpose is rotation of players toward the side that the offense is hitting the ball. The weakness of this defense is that it leaves the middle back of the court open. Like the perimeter defense, it shifts players to cover the more common left side hits, too.

GLOSSARY

attack line (uh TAK LYN) — a line on the court marking 9 feet 10 inches (3 meters) away from the net running from sideline to sideline

attacker: (uh TAK er) — the player responsible for receiving a set and attacking; a hitter

back court (BAK KAWRT) — the area of the court between the attack line and the baseline

block (BLAHK) — the act of stopping a spiked ball, performed by front court players, with hands up and outstretched

defensive formations (di FEN siv fawr MAY shunz) — any arrangement of players for receiving serves or attacks; such as the 2-1-3 and the 2-4

dig (DIG) — receiving an attack with a forearm pass, usually low in the back court

emergency technique (uh MER jen see TEK NEEK) — motion that involves falling to the floor to receive an out-of-range ball; see "Dive," "Roll," and "Sprawl"

forearm pass (FAWR AHRM PAS) — the basic passing technique using the forearms as the contact area

free ball formation (FREE BAWL fawr MAY shun) — the standard defensive position players move into when no formation is called

GLOSSARY

front court (FRUNT KAWRT) — area of the court between the net and the attack line

multiple offense (MUL tuh pul AHF ens) — any offensive formation usually placing the setter in the back court

overhead pass (O ver HED PAS) — the basic passing technique using both hands and overhead motion

set (SET) — a pass that prepares the ball for the hitter to attack

setter (SET er) — the player responsible for setting the ball to the hitter

simple offense (SIM pul AHF ENS) — any offensive formation that places the setter in the front court

tip (TIP) — an off-speed attack; a dink

U formation (YOO fawr MAY shun) — a serve reception formation in which the players are positioned in a "U" pattern on the court.

W formation (DUB ul yoo fawr MAY shun) — a serve reception formation in which the players are positioned in a "W" pattern on the court

FURTHER READING

Find out more with these helpful books and information sites:

American Coaching Effectiveness Program, Rookie Coaches Volleyball Guide. Champagne, IL: Human Kinetics, 1993.

Howard, Robert E. *An Understanding of the Fundamental Techniques of Volleyball.* Needham Heights, MA: Allyn and Bacon, 1996.

Kluka, Darlene, and Dunn, Peter. *Volleyball.* Wm. C. Brown, 1996.

Neville, William S. *Coaching Volleyball Successfully.* New York: Leisure, 1990.

Vierra, Barbara, and Ferguson, Bonnie Jill. *Volleyball: Steps to Success.* Human Kinetics, 1996.

American Volleyball Coaches Association at
http://www.volleyball.org/avca/index.html

Complete worldwide source for volleyball information at
http://www.volleyball.org/
This site includes descriptions and ordering information for many new books and videos; also, many links.

Great links: http://users.aol.com/vballusa/index.htm

Online Volleyball Magazine subscription page at
http://www.volleyballmag.com/sub.htm

More volleyball information at http://www.volleyball.com

INDEX